The Fantastic Adventures of Krishna
©Demi, 2013

For children of all ages in
Krishna's Universal Dance

Book design by Stephen Williams

The illustrations are rendered in mixed media

Wisdom Tales is an imprint of World Wisdom, Inc.

Library of Congress Cataloging-in-Publication Data

Demi.
  The fantastic adventures of Krishna / written and illustrated by Demi.
      pages cm
  ISBN 978-1-937786-05-2 (hardcover : alk. paper) I. Krishna (Hindu deity)--Juvenile
literature. I. Title.
  BL1220.D46 2013
  294.5'2113--dc23

                                                                        2012041254

Printed in China on acid-free paper
Production Date: December 2012, Plant & Location: Printed by Everbest Printing (Guangzhou, China),
Co. Ltd, Job / Batch: # 111282

For information address Wisdom Tales,
P.O. Box 2682, Bloomington, Indiana 47402-2682
www.wisdomtalespress.com

THE FANTASTIC ADVENTURES OF KRISHNA

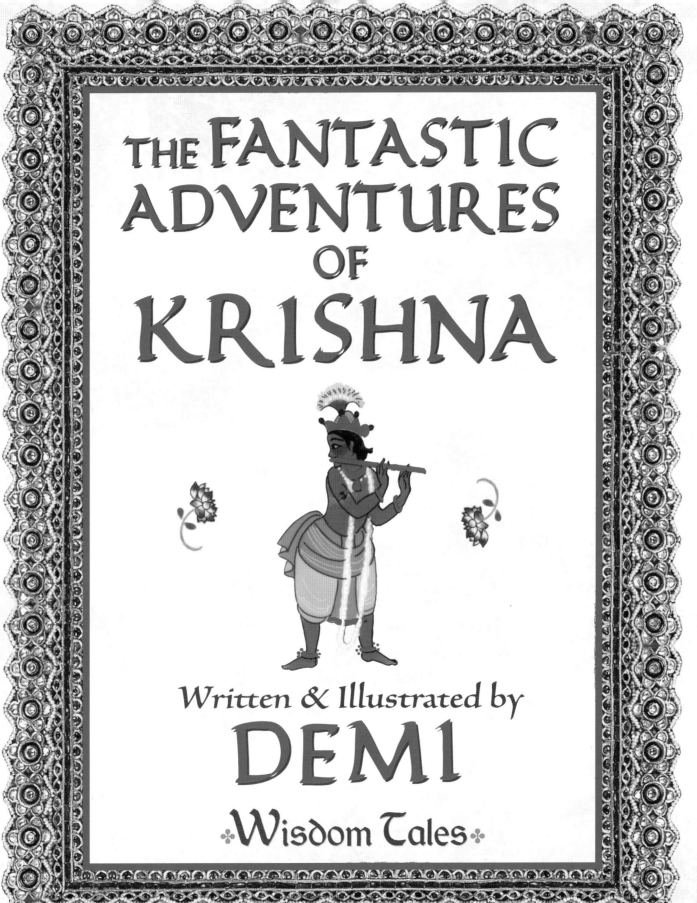

Written & Illustrated by

DEMI

Wisdom Tales

Over five thousand years ago, in the land of India, ruled a wise and just king named Ugrasena.

E verywhere there was peace, joy, and love.

But evil demon kings were killing all the good rulers on the earth.

The people worshiped Mother Earth as a goddess named Bhumi. She was very upset by the deaths.

In the form of a sacred cow, she went to the heaven of Lord Vishnu, the greatest of all the gods. With her came Lord Brahma, creator of the universe, and many other gods. Together they all begged Lord Vishnu for his help.

Lord Vishnu said, "Do not worry. I will be reborn on earth as a child named Krishna. I will destroy all the evil demon kings and bring peace once again to the earth."

B ut the kingdom
had already been
overthrown by an evil
demon king named Kamsa.
He had the good King
Ugrasena placed in prison.
   Kamsa even put his own
sister and her husband in
prison. He was certain that
their future son, Krishna,
would one day kill him
and make the earth
peaceful again.
   The evil king was ready
and waiting to kill the
newborn son.

On the night that
Krishna was born, a
great miracle happened.
  The guards fell into
a deep sleep. Then the
prison gates opened all by
themselves!
  The baby Krishna was
carried out of the prison
and given to two cowherds,
Yashoda and Nanda.
They loved the baby as
their own.

In the morning there was great celebration among the cowherds. News spread that Yashoda and Nanda had a son named Krishna.

King Kamsa was very angry. He sent an evil demon to kill Krishna. Disguised as an old servant lady, the demon pretended to help the child. But little Krishna saw that it was evil. He quickly used his powers to take away the life inside it.

K ing Kamsa was furious. He decided to send something worse—a whirlwind demon!

But, by using all his great powers, Krishna easily destroyed this mighty demon too.

King Kamsa returned in defeat to his palace and left Krishna in peace.

Krishna was growing up to be a clever, adorable, but naughty child. He loved butter, and would take it from every house in the neighborhood.

One day, his adopted mother Yashoda tied him to a stone as punishment. It was so heavy that ten men together could not lift it.

But Krishna crawled across the fields, pulling the heavy stone behind him. When it became caught between two huge trees, he gave an extra tug, and pulled the trees down.

Everyone was amazed by the strength of the little child Krishna.

Hearing stories of Krishna's great powers made King Kamsa more fearful than ever.

He decided to send his crane demon to eat young Krishna as he was herding cows.

The bird snapped Krishna into its beak, and was ready to swallow him. But Krishna magically caused his body to become hot. This forced the crane demon to spit him out.

Then Krishna broke the crane's beak, defeating the evil bird.

King Kamsa was greatly worried by Krishna's incredible power. He next sent a giant eight-mile-long snake demon to eat up the cowherds.

The snake opened its mouth wide. Its chin touched the ground and its nose touched the sky. Its mouth looked just like a mountain cave, and its sharp teeth looked like rocks.

The other young cowherds were curious. They crawled inside the open mouth to play.

But Krishna ran inside the demon's throat, and with his special powers began to grow bigger and bigger.

The great snake choked and coughed, causing all the cowherds to fly out of its mouth.

As Krishna's victories increased, evil King Kamsa grew more and more jealous.

He decided to send Agni, the god of fire, to defeat Krishna.

One day Agni came to earth and created a huge forest fire. This, he thought, would surely kill Krishna, the cowherds, and all the cows.

But Krishna stopped Agni. He quickly sucked up all the flames and put them out in his mouth!

B ecause of all the evil demons,
   Krishna's family decided to move.
They chose a faraway place called
Vrindavana.
   And so everyone packed up their
belongings and headed for safety.

The fields of Vrindavana were beautiful. Along the grassy paths, fig trees bloomed. Delightful birds of every color sang from their branches.

Flowers grew everywhere and the air smelled like perfume. The boys would sing together and Krishna would play his flute. When they heard this, the cows would run and play and the peacocks would dance!

Krishna, his older brother Balarama, and the cowherds would play hide-and-seek in the woods. They would practice with their slingshots and wrestle one another.

Some days Krishna, Balarama, and the cowherds would walk along the banks of the river. Wild geese and ducks splashed about, and fish swam among the yellow lotus flowers.

Other days the boys would dive in and swim with the elephants. The gentle creatures would spray them with water from their trunks.

Everyone felt as happy as if they were in Vishnu's paradise.

By now King Kamsa had learned where Krishna was living.

He decided to send another snake demon to Krishna's favorite swimming place.

But Krishna noticed that the water had become still. All the birds and animals had vanished.

He knew the black snake must be near. So he dived into the water to fight him.

The king of snakes sprang out of the water. Its giant body was ready to strike.

Out of its many mouths shot flames and smoke. It seemed as if they would destroy the whole world.

The powerful snake tried to wrap itself around Krishna and bite him with its poisonous fangs. But Krishna leapt on the snake demon's head and began to dance victoriously. Through his miraculous powers, all the snake's fire and poison vanished. It was defeated.

Every year the cowherds went to a sacred mountain to worship Indra, the god of rain.

But Krishna said they should worship the mountain, forest, and cattle deities instead. He said that they brought greater blessings.

The god Indra was greatly upset by this. He sent heavy rain that threatened the cowherds and their cattle.

But Krishna, with a single finger, lifted up the whole mountain.

For seven days he held it up, sheltering everyone from the rain.

Indra realized that Krishna had within him all the powers of Vishnu, Lord of the universe. So Indra bowed down before him.

Indra praised Krishna by calling him *Govinda*, "Lord of the cows." Indra then caused heavenly rain and flowers to fall from the sky.

Everyone worshiped Krishna as their divine protector. The cowgirls loved him deeply, and Krishna rejoiced, dancing and singing.

Krishna remained a huge threat to King Kamsa. He began to realize that the all-powerful God Vishnu must have been reborn as the child Krishna!

This thought made him very afraid. But he came up with yet another plot to destroy Krishna.

He decided to trick Krishna into coming to the kingdom's great athletic festival.

He knew that Krishna and his brother Balarama would try to win the wrestling contest.

But secretly he planned their deaths.

The great stadium was decorated with flags of many colors. But before Krishna and Balarama could enter it, King Kamsa set his demon elephant upon them.

The maddened elephant, with its snakelike trunk, rushed forward.

K rishna leapt high into the air. For one hour he played with the gigantic elephant as if it were a toy.

Finally, the exhausted creature fell on its knees. Krishna pulled out one of its tusks and killed the demon elephant with it.

Furious, King Kamsa yelled, "Kill the parents of Krishna and Balarama. Kill the parents of all the cowherds!"

Krishna stood silent, gathering all the power of the universe within himself.

Then, with one huge leap, he jumped from the stadium floor to King Kamsa's high seat. Like lightning, Krishna grabbed Kamsa's hair in his iron grip. He dragged the king face down into the arena.

Around and around Krishna went,
until the evil king gasped his last
breath and died.

The whole arena erupted in joy.

The parents of Krishna and Balarama were freed from prison and were joyously reunited with their sons. The good King Ugrasena was freed from prison, too, and he was put back on the throne.

Krishna said to the people of the kingdom, "Everything I have done has been for the peace of the world. For my sake, fill the days and nights of your life with love for all beings. Rejoice, for I shall always be with you in my thoughts."

With that, Krishna left. He went far and wide helping all of humankind and showing them how to live together in peace and joy.